AF270123

Dogs & More Dogs!

BOOKS OUT LOUD COLLECTION

Dogs & More Dogs!

by Grace Hansen

Welcome to BOOKS OUT LOUD!
This one-of-a-kind collection consists
of twelve wildly popular Abdo Zoom titles,
the bestselling classroom favorites. Get ready
to feed your brain with the same amazing
Abdo Read-to-Me experience kids know and
love at school—and become a powerhouse
reader anytime, anywhere.

Please scan the QR code on the back cover to
link to the accompanying audio, or visit
www.Downpour.com/dogs-and-more-dogs

Contents

Australian Shepherds

by Grace Hansen

Table of Contents

Australian Shepherds

In the 1800s, Basque shepherds came to the United States from Australia. They brought dogs with them. These dogs later became the Australian shepherd breed.

Australian shepherds
began as skilled farm
and ranch dogs. Today,
Aussies also work as
guide and therapy
dogs. Others are
police or rescue dogs.

SERVICE
IN TRAIN
DO NOT

Aussies are medium-sized dogs. They have strong legs and muscular bodies.

Aussies have long,
wavy or straight hair.
They come in many
beautiful colors.

Aussies can be black, red, or blueish in color. Some have a merle coat pattern. They may also have white or tan markings.

An Aussie's eyes can be brown, blue, or amber. Some Aussies have two different colored eyes. One eye can also have specks of different colors.

Grooming

Aussies need to be brushed weekly. This will keep their coats healthy. It will also help with shedding.

Exercise

Aussies can live in the city but are happiest with a large yard. They need lots of exercise. Once they are done growing, they make great jogging buddies.

Personality

Aussies are wonderful family pets. They are smart, easy to train, and loyal. Besides love and care, they need a job to do!

More Facts

- Many Australian shepherds still herd cattle today in the American West.

- A healthy Australian shepherd can live for 12 to 15 years.

- Australian shepherds belong to the herding group of dog breeds. This means they have the ability to control the movement of other animals.

Glossary

Basque shepherd – a person known for expert shepherding from the borderlands between France and Spain. In the early 1800s, many Basques travelled to Australia with their dogs to herd sheep, and later sailed to California where ranchers were introduced to their amazing dogs.

breed – a particular type of animal.

loyal – showing devotion and faithfulness to someone.

merle – a coat pattern that creates patches of color.

shed – to give off hair.

therapy dog – a dog that goes with its owner to visit people in order to bring comfort or cheer. Therapy dogs are different from service dogs, which are specially trained to perform specific tasks.

Chihuahuas

by Grace Hansen

Photo Credits: iStock, Shutterstock, Thinkstock

Production Contributors: Teddy Borth, Jennie Forsberg, Grace Hansen
Design Contributors: Dorothy Toth, Pakou Moua

Table of Contents

Chihuahuas

Chihuahuas are a very old dog breed. They were named in the mid-1800s after Chihuahua, Mexico. However, they have been popular pets for hundreds of years.

United States
Mexico
Chihuahua

Chihuahuas are the smallest dog breed. They weigh less than 6 pounds (3 kg). They are just 6 to 9 inches (15-23 cm) tall.

A Chihuahua's head
is small and round.
Its ears are large and
stand up on its head.
The dog's eyes are
full, round, and set
far apart.

Chihuahuas can have long or short coats. The coats can be many colors including fawn, red, black, and white. They can also have markings.

Grooming

Chihuahuas with long coats should be brushed weekly. All Chihuahuas should be bathed around once a month.

Exercise

Chihuahuas prefer shorter walks. But they can handle longer walks at a slower pace.

Personality

Though tiny in size, Chihuahuas have big personalities. They are also very smart and sensitive. They respond well to gentle training.

Chihuahuas are very attached to their owners. They like to go wherever their owners go.

Chihuahuas are tough pups. But they are physically small and fragile. Their families should always handle them with care.

More Facts

- Dogs resembling Chihuahuas can be found in ancient paintings in Mexico.

- The El Paso Chihuahuas are a minor league baseball team located in El Paso, Texas. Their mascot is Chico, a tough Chihuahua!

- *Beverly Hills Chihuahua* is a 2008 comedy film that follows the adventures of Chihuahuas Chloe and Papi.

Glossary

ancient – very old.

breed – a particular type of animal.

fawn – yellowish tan.

fragile – easily hurt.

sensitive – highly aware or feeling things strongly.

Dachshunds

by Grace Hansen

Photo Credits: Alamy, iStock, Minden Pictures, Shutterstock, Thinkstock

Production Contributors: Teddy Borth, Jennie Forsberg, Grace Hansen
Design Contributors: Dorothy Toth, Pakou Moua

Table of Contents

Dachshunds

Dachshunds are as cute as they are long! But they were not bred to be cute.

Pronounced dahks-hund, the dog's name is made up of two German words. *Dachs* is German for badger. *Hund* means dog.

These dogs were bred more than 600 years ago. Their main job was to hunt badgers. Badgers are tough animals. But the small, sturdy dachshund is tougher!

Dachshunds have low, long bodies. They are the perfect size and shape to get into badger dens.

Dachshunds come in two sizes. Standard dachshunds are 8 to 9 inches (20 to 23 cm) tall. Minis are 5 to 6 inches (13 to 15 cm) tall.

Dachshunds have three coat types. Smooth coats are short and soft. They are easy to groom and keep clean.

longhaired
wire
smooth

Longhaired dachshunds
were bred for places
with cooler weather.
Dogs with wire coats
can hunt in places
with dense or thorny
surroundings. The wiry
hair protects the skin.

Dachshunds' coats can be many colors, like red, black, cream, and tan. They can also have different markings.

Personality

Dachshunds were bred to be independent hunters. However, they are still social and want to be with their families. Their bold personalities and sweet faces make them easy to love.

More Facts

- Dachshunds tend to live longer than many dog breeds. Most live 12 to 15 years.

- A dachshund named Chanel once held the title of oldest-living dog. She lived to be 21 years old!

- Dachshunds are members of the American Kennel Club (AKC) Hound Group. They are the group's smallest members!

Glossary

bred – developed over time for a certain purpose.

dense – thick and hard to see through or move through.

independent – not needing the support of another.

sturdy – strong, hardy, or solid.

wire – firm and stiff.

German Shorthaired Pointers

by Grace Hansen

Table of Contents

German Shorthaired Pointers

Both kind and smart, the German shorthaired pointer makes a great companion.

Breeders worked for years to create the perfect hunting dog. And they succeeded!

The German shorthaired pointer is named for where it was bred. "Shorthaired" is for the dog's short, thick, and tough coat. And the natural-born hunter stops and points when it finds its prey.

German shorthaireds
are medium-sized
dogs. They can grow
up to 35 inches
(89 cm) high. They
can weigh up to 70
pounds (32 kg).

German shorthaireds
can be many colors,
including black, liver,
white, and roan. They
have patchy markings.

Grooming

A German shorthaired's ears should be cleaned regularly. The dog only needs a bath every now and then.

Exercise

German shorthaireds need regular exercise. Hunting gives dogs plenty of work to do. Going on long runs and playing fetch are other good forms of exercise.

German shorthaireds are also great swimmers. Their webbed toes help them move in the water. They can either swim for fun or fetch downed ducks!

Personality

German shorthaireds learn quickly and are eager to please. Their intelligence needs to be matched with activity. This all-purpose hunting dog loves its family and a job to do!

More Facts

- German shorthaired pointers (GSPs) are good swimmers. They have webbed feet and strong, sleek bodies.

- GSPs can compete in and dominate almost any dog sport.

- While GSPs have short coats, they can shed a lot. Weekly brushing can help.

Glossary

bred – developed over time for a certain purpose.

breeder – one whose job it is to breed animals.

companion – one who spends time with another or others.

eager – wanting very much.

intelligence – the ability to learn or understand.

roan – having a dark coat thickly sprinkled with white.

thick – having parts that are very close together.

Pembroke Welsh Corgis

by Grace Hansen

Table of Contents

Pembroke Welsh Corgis

The Pembroke Welsh corgi is from Pembrokeshire. Pembrokeshire is in Wales, a country in the United Kingdom.

United Kingdom
Wales
Europe

N
W
E
S

The Pembroke corgi's roots go back to the early 1100s. It was then that two kinds of dogs were brought to Wales. From them, the Pembroke corgi was bred.

Pembroke corgis
were bred to work
on farms. They were
trained to herd
birds like geese and
chickens. They could
also rid farms of rats
and other pests.

Corgis could also herd larger animals, like pigs and cattle. The dogs would nip at the animals' heels. Their short height helped them avoid being kicked.

Pembroke corgis are small and sturdy. They stand just 10 to 12 inches (25-30 cm) tall. They weigh around 30 pounds (14 kg).

Pembroke corgis have pointed ears. Their tails are docked. Their legs are short but powerful.

Their coats are medium in length. They can be red, sable, fawn, black, or tan in color. They can have white markings.

Exercise

Corgis need exercise every day. Daily walks and play are important. They also need firm but kind training.

Personality

Corgis are smart and strong willed. They are also loving without being too needy. The dog's fun personality and cheerful face make owning one fun!

More Facts

- Queen Elizabeth II's favorite pups in the world are Pembroke Welsh corgis. She has owned more than 30 in her lifetime.

- Though both called corgis, the Pembroke Welsh corgi and the Cardigan Welsh corgi are two separate breeds.

- Pembrokes are good watch dogs. They will bark if anyone or anything comes near their homes.

Glossary

bred – developed over time for a certain purpose.

breed – a particular type of animal.

docked – shortened.

fawn – yellowish tan.

roots – family background.

sable – very dark.

sturdy – strong, hardy, or solid.

Siberian Huskies

by Grace Hansen

Table of Contents

Siberian Huskies

Siberian huskies are as outgoing as they are loyal.

The Siberian husky's ancestors **were** **bred** in Asia by the Chukchi people. The Chukchi people kept these dogs as family members and tough sled dogs.

The Chukchi people
were semi nomadic.
They moved from
place to place,
especially to hunt.
They needed a dog
that could haul heavy
loads in very cold
temperatures.

From these dogs came the Siberian huskies we know and love today. In the early 1900s, husky teams won many dog sled races. They caught the attention of people everywhere.

Siberian huskies are medium-sized working dogs. They are known for their beautiful fur coats and bright eyes.

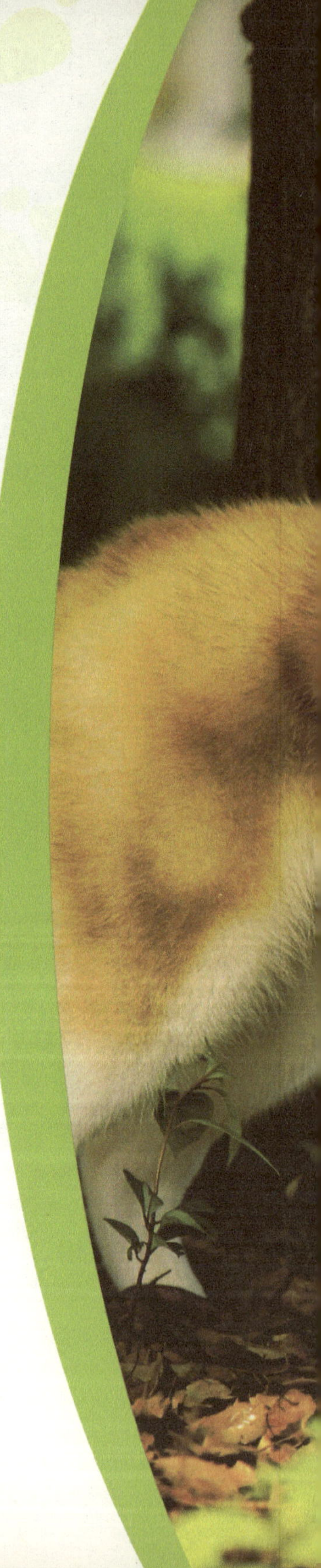

Their ears stand up straight. Their eyes can be brown or blue. They can sometimes have one eye of each color!

Grooming

Huskies are naturally clean. They only need to be bathed every 3 months or so. They should be brushed regularly to keep their coats healthy.

Exercise

Siberian huskies are energetic and athletic. It is important that they get lots of exercise. Born to run, they are happiest doing that with their owners.

Personality

Pack dogs by nature, Siberian huskies love their families and other pets. They are a great addition to any team!

More Facts

- A husky's almond-shaped eyes allow the dog to squint to keep the snow out while running. Its thick, double coat keeps the dog nice and warm.

- Huskies are heroes of history. In 1925, children living in Nome, Alaska, became very sick. They needed medicine that was hundreds of miles away. It was decided that multiple dogsled teams would get the medicine to Nome.

- Two famous Siberian huskies on that life-saving run were Balto and Togo. Balto is more well-known. He ran the last 55 miles (89 km) to Nome. But Togo and his team ran the most dangerous leg of the journey. Togo's musher said, "I never had a better dog than Togo."

Glossary

ancestor – an early type of animal from which others have evolved.

bred – developed over time for a certain purpose.

Chukchi – indigenous people inhabiting the northeastern most part of Siberia in Russia.

loyal – showing devotion and faithfulness to someone.

musher – one who travels with a dog team.

nomadic – living in a group or tribe that moves from place to place.

Beagles

by Grace Hansen

Table of Contents

Beagles

Beagles are quick and curious. They have an excellent sense of smell. Beagles follow their noses wherever they go!

Beagles are small but sturdy hound dogs. They are about 1 foot (30.5 cm) tall at the shoulders. They have long, pointed tails.

Beagles have round, brown or hazel eyes. They have floppy ears. Their noses are black.

Beagles can be any hound color. But the tricolor beagle is the most common. Tricolor beagles are white, tan, and black.

A beagle's smooth, dense coat is rain resistant. Its coat is thicker in winter. This makes for lots of fur!

Grooming & Exercise

Beagles shed, but not too much. Brushing them weekly will help. Cleaning their ears regularly is important, too.

Beagles need their exercise. They love to go on daily brisk walks. Beagles must be leashed. If they pick up a scent, they will follow it!

Food & Play

Beagles love to eat. Their noses lead them to tasty treats. Food and garbage should be kept out of reach.

Beagles do not like to

be alone for too long.

They are friendly, fun,

and love to play. So

lots of time with their

families is important!

More Facts

- Beagles do not make the usual barking sound. It is more like a quick, short howl.

- Beagles were first bred to track rabbits and hares. They are still used for this today.

- Beagles are often used for security purposes. Their sense of smell is amazing. But they are also very cute and friendly! So people feel comfortable around them.

Glossary

curious – eager to learn or know.

dense – having parts that are close together.

hazel – a color that combines brown, green, and gray.

resistant – capable of withstanding the effect of something.

sturdy – strongly built.

Boxers

by Grace Hansen

Photo Credits: iStock, Shutterstock, Thinkstock

Production Contributors: Teddy Borth, Jennie Forsberg, Grace Hansen

Design Contributors: Dorothy Toth, Laura Mitchell

Table of Contents

Boxers

Like human boxers, these dogs move smoothly and powerfully. They are also fearless!

Boxers are medium-sized dogs. They weigh 60 to 70 pounds (27 to 32 kg).

Boxers have wrinkled foreheads and muzzles. They have dark brown eyes. Their ears naturally lie flat. Some boxers have cropped ears.

Boxers are born with
long tails. Some have
their tails docked
after birth.

A boxer's coat is short
and shiny. It fits tight
on the body.

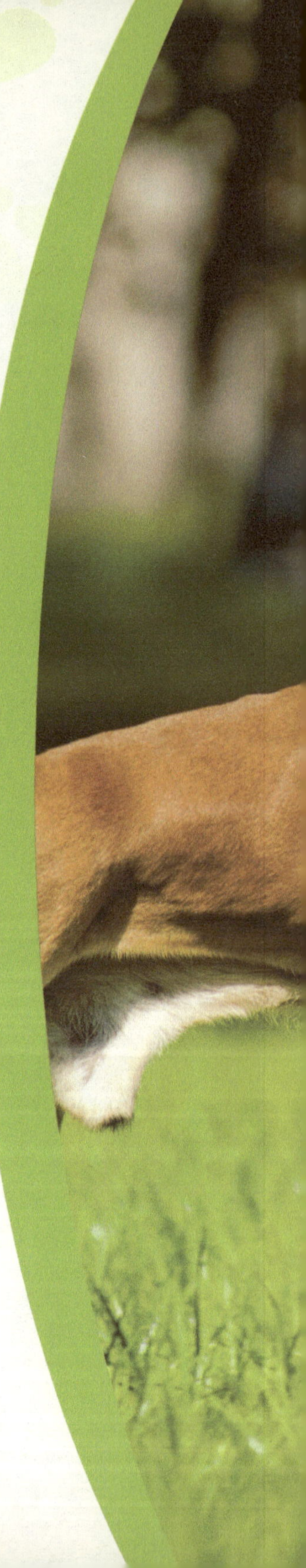

Boxer coats can be brindle or fawn. They can have white markings. All boxers have black masks on their faces.

Grooming

Boxers are clean dogs due to their short coats. They need only an occasional bath. Boxers shed, so brushing them weekly will help. Cleaning their ears is also important.

Exercise & Play

Boxers are very active. They need lots of exercise. Boxers love going for long walks or jogs. They also enjoy playing fetch.

Personality

Boxers are very smart and easy to train. They are also kind and playful. Boxers are loving members of their families.

More Facts

- Boxers are loving and protective, which makes them popular dogs for families.

- The Boxer finds its beginnings in Germany. Its ancestors were made for hunting and holding prey, and later as guard dogs.

- The original reason for Boxers' docked tails and cropped ears was so the animals they were hunting could not grab onto them. Fewer of today's Boxer owners dock or crop their dogs.

Glossary

brindle – having dark streaks or spots on a gray, tan, or tawny background.

cropped – made to stick straight up.

docked – made to be shorter.

muzzle – part of a dog's face that includes the nose and mouth.

smoothly – even and uninterrupted in flow.

French Bulldogs

by Grace Hansen

Table of Contents

French Bulldogs

French Bulldogs are also called "Frenchies." They are as sweet as they are cute!

Frenchies are small and sturdy. They have strong legs. Their hind legs are longer than their front legs.

Frenchies have big, square heads. They have flat, round faces. Their muzzles are short and wrinkled.

Frenchies have round

eyes. Their ears

are round and stick

straight up!

Frenchies have short, shiny coats. They come in many colors. Many frenchies have markings.

Care & Exercise

Frenchies are easy to care for. They only need to be brushed once a week. Cleaning between their wrinkles is also important.

Frenchies do
not need a lot of
exercise. One brisk
walk a day will do.

It is hard for Frenchies
to breathe in the heat.
If it is a very hot day,
they should play inside.

Companions

Frenchies love to play and have fun. They also love just to be near their humans. They make good watchdogs and friends!

More Facts

- Frenchies are known for their snorting. They snort because of their short muzzles.

- Frenchie tails come in all shapes and sizes. Some are very short and some are a little longer. At any length, they can be straight or curved.

- The French bulldog's beginnings are actually in England, not France. But the friendly little dog was very popular in France. So, they named the dog after the country.

Glossary

brisk – quick.

hind – back; rear.

marking – a mark or pattern of marks on an animal's fur.

muzzle – part of a dog's face that includes the nose and mouth.

sturdy – strongly built.

Great Danes

by Grace Hansen

Table of Contents

Great Danes

The Great Dane is one of the tallest dog breeds. It can grow nearly 3 feet (1 m) tall!

Everything about the
Great Dane is big. It
has long legs and a
long tail. Its head is
very large.

Great Danes have large ears. Some are cropped, while others are folded over. Their paws can be as big as human hands!

The Great Dane's body is muscular. It is covered in short, shiny hair.

Great Danes come in many colors. They can also have **markings**.

Care & Exercise

Great Danes shed a lot. Brushing them often will help. An occasional bath is also needed.

Great Danes do not
need a lot of exercise.
They'd rather lie on
the couch! But, a
few walks a day are
important.

Great Danes need high quality dog food. A raised food bowl is also needed. Proper feeding will keep them healthy!

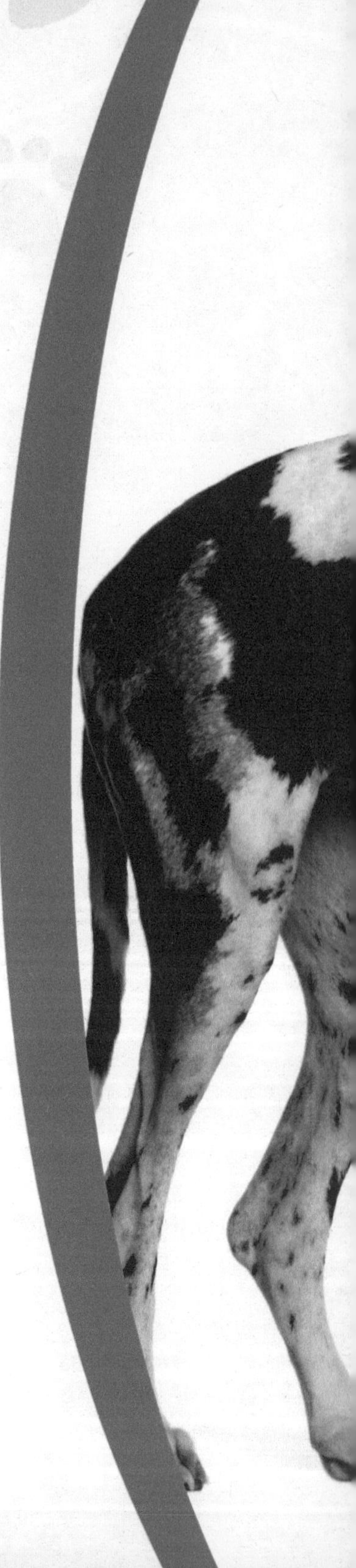

Gentle Giants

Great Danes can look scary! But they are very gentle. They are good with kids. They are loving members of their families!

More Facts

- Great Danes will nudge owners with their big heads when they want attention!

- These big dogs easily get cold. A dog coat is nice for walks in cold winter months.

- Because of its size, the Great Dane has a very short life expectancy. Great Danes usually live between 7.5 and 10 years.

Glossary

breed – a certain kind of dog.

cropped – made to stick straight up.

high quality – the best.

marking – a mark or pattern of marks on an animal's fur.

muscular – strong and athletic.

Poodles

by Grace Hansen

Table of Contents

Poodles

Poodles can look a little snooty. But in fact, poodles are very friendly. They are also known for being silly!

Poodles come in
three sizes. They are
standard, miniature,
and toy. Standard
poodles are the
largest. Toy poodles
are the smallest.

standard

miniature

toy

Poodles have thick,
curly coats. Their
coats come in many
colors. Common
colors include apricot,
gray, and white.

apricot   **gray**    **white**

Grooming & Exercise

Poodles do not shed a lot. However, their curly coats easily become matted. They should be trimmed every four to six weeks.

Standard poodles tend
to be more active.
They need to run and
play. Having a job to
do makes them happy.

All poodles need
exercise. A daily walk
is important. More
active games, like
fetch, are fun too!

Brains & Personality

All poodles are very smart. They are easy to train. They like learning new tricks!

Poodles do not like

being alone for long.

They are happiest with

their families.

Poodles do well with other pets. Most poodles are good with kids. All poodle owners agree that poodles are the best!

More Facts

- Poodles are very good swimmers. Poodle comes from the German word *pudeln*, meaning "to splash."

- In France, poodles were known for their hunting abilities. Hunters used them to retrieve ducks from water.

- Poodles are one of the smartest dog breeds.

Glossary

matted – formed into a tangled mass.

snooty – showing the attitude that one is better, smarter, or more important than others.

Scottish Terriers

by Grace Hansen

Photo Credits: Animal Photography, AP Images, iStock, Shutterstock, Thinkstock, © Grace Hansen (feat. Louie) p.4

Production Contributors: Teddy Borth, Jennie Forsberg, Grace Hansen

Design Contributors: Dorothy Toth, Laura Mitchell

Table of Contents

Scottish Terriers

Scottish terriers are also called "Scotties." Scotties have strong features, big personalities, and deep barks. They are hard to miss!

Scotties have pointed
ears and tails. They
have short, strong
legs. Their sturdy
bodies are covered
in wiry hair.

Scotties come in six colors. But there are three main colors. They are black, brindle, and wheaten.

black

brindle

wheaten

Grooming

Scotties should be brushed often. Their wiry hair easily tangles. They need regular trips to the groomer.

Many Scotties wear
the classic cut.
This includes long
eyebrows and a beard.
The hair is also kept
long around the legs.

Walk & Play

Scotties love daily, fast walks. They must always be leashed. This keeps them safe.

Scotties have a strong instinct to chase things. They love having their toys thrown for them to run after. Their other favorite game is tug-of-war!

Personality

Scotties are smart and confident. They think their way is the right way. So, training them can be hard. Treats usually get them to work with you.

Scotties are never shy. They are always loyal and loving. But they can have an odd way of showing it!

More Facts

- Four Scottish terriers have lived in the White House. Fala and Meggie belonged to Franklin D. Roosevelt. Barney and Miss Beazley were George W. Bush's Scotties.

- Scottish terriers have the second most wins at the Westminster Kennel Club Dog Show. By 2015, Scotties had won Best in Show eight times!

- Scotties have their beginnings in Scotland. Farmers and hunters used Scotties to hunt rodents, badgers, foxes, and other animals.

Glossary

confident – sure of oneself.

feature – a characteristic belonging to a thing and serving to identify it.

instinct – natural feeling.

sturdy – strongly built.

wiry – firm and stiff.